# Harness Bells

# Harness Bells

## Poems

### Dick Heaberlin

Orange House Books

San Marcos, Texas

For additional information, visit the author's
website at DickHeaberlinWrites.com.

ISBN 978-0-9794964-7-9

For my son David

# Contents

# Harness Bells

Harness bells?

Yes,

big and solid    brass and leather

out of place

and time

harness bells

in Shelby in central Texas

in October

in an antique dealer's booth

many strings of them

light sounds

strings strongly leather

the sounds of warm smells

of heated horses

in blue air

the surprisingly light sounds of purpose

the going and getting there

the strength of

Percherons, Belgians, and Clydesdales

a way never known by me yet known.

Yes, they jingle of icy slices of wind

warm clothes

maybe an old patchwork quilt in the lap

just like the one in the next booth

in warm Shelby

in Central Texas

in October.

# Hardwood

Been cutting on that tree
about a life
little change —
hard wood.

I like cutting
going to keep it up
hands a bit sore
knife's not sharp
people been nodding
shaking their heads
watching me cut
going away.

I stay at it
glad they're gone
keeping on.

One fellow said,
"Man, you crazy."
no smile
me neither
on and on.

Another said
"You cut that tree,
you be famous."
maybe,

but

I have committed right
and wish to admit my true
for chameleons know sure
one tree when we are old
running about roots in wile
and heat, wise into the way
of phloem and xylem
we seekers of hardwood
with a small knife.

# Being with Angels

Mary Ann
scratches
a green pirate
from her palette
in short breaths
her own all
her ecstasy, her despair
her green, her pirate,
her knowing of her Picasso, her Rodin,
her Cassatt, her mères and pères,
her soeurs and frères
she and them and pirate and green — one
in short breaths
her eyes arrows
her fingers arrows
flying
her mind commanding
"there, now, again, there, and there
that much, no, more"
flying
to clink against adamant

Mary Ann
like Gauguin's Jacob
wrestling an angel
wrestling with the possible
having to sort, choose, grab, want, will
and settling at lasts
for what she's got —
a hank of hair
smelling
of angel sweat.

# Epitaph

He went out
to find out
what there was out there
to find out
out there
and he did
and he died.

# Writing

Words scrawled
by dull sticks
quickened by sharp thoughts
can come slow
like old smooth-mouthed horses
moving to a dark stall
blanketed and blinkered by night
to stand still stopped by age's
tight hand with reins
to a bit of steel

or

can clatter
about
like racing colts
romp stout
without oughts
frisky, prissy
loose and running
rippling.

# Release Lightning

I'd pamper the anvil.
I'd burnish it,
get some hard glow,
scuffle with
hammered stars,
release lightning
crisp through
blue air,
bend with flame and wind
blended hot
the hard things,
get along
into shaping shapes
making parts,
even into
tiger hearts,
do it
sweating,
humming,
swearing.

# Mountain Wren

Toughly,
on brushy perch,
the diminutive wren
marks his land,
his throat exploding notes
to mingle with the distant tones of hawk.
While I observe him strut and sing,
the sun drops through shaky aspen leaves,
upon my back,
coldly flecking me —
black and white —
wren spotted,
and such a singer I would be,
had I his throat, his aplomb.

# Embers

I have taken

Cezanne's apples —

red,

lined in black —

from the table

and have them in my night —

coals

to warm my hands against.

                              /
                         fa
                    me
               re
          do
     laˇ

# Simul-
## taneous-
### ly

From wood
Brancusi cut
the comb
and crow
of a
cock.
What color
the sound
he touched?
The size of the thought
that dawned?
How chill
the trill
that into the sky
unfurled!

# Derring-do, Devant de Dada

le bateau ivre

(On Feb. 15, 1913, the home of the regiment)

Few dare to see the light
that eats the golden pear

dare to breathe
  bro ken
the light
in

dare walk the stair

naked

dare
redeSIGNate

their part

dare

float drunk

                    in a drunken boat

# The Matter with Ophelia

She would know

would scour dawn

look into the banty's eye

approach the edge

through a field

of weeds

lie in the dew

gather beggar's lice

in her knotted hair

hear the beat

of the great blue heron

hum ditties

# Controlling Cold

he gave

sent out

a bit

from him

of some warm thing

when cold

was controlling

she felt

the bit

shivered less

but cold is firm

and long

he knew

and  she

through nights

of knowledge

love

cold

# To Take Ten

I ache
to ride light
on a lake of wind

to beat
meagerly
seldom

snuggle soft
a bubble
in a cloud
then to twitch

shake hard all
latch firm
to wind song
and swerve
a curve
of swoop
Oh!

to feel the swing
of go.

# Panentheism

—we come

to be with Light,

slowly,

deeply,

in admiration,

for comprehension —

we would know,

know It, us,

come to be

Us —

# Red Peg

Up there, on the surface of the Sun,
The Fire Beast grazes on gaseous plains,
sometimes exploding into fiery fury,
shaking her flaxen mane and sending rays
deep into space.  Ripples of her sorrel
shoulders swirl tornadic energy away —
white blasts arcing out.  Her hooves
strike sparks as riderless she bows
her back, bucking torches toward us.
Then the Fire Beast relents, rests,
as if hobbled, eared down, twitched.
Yet the eyes of the steed still flash fire
and the heart pumps lava about. Temporarily
timid and tamed she refrains from releasing
the cataclysmic blasts, dear old Peg.

# Hobo and Yoyo

It's nice to ride the trotting earth

a flick of sun on face

then neck

like a hobo in a boxcar on a freight train

heading west

wind in the hair

or like a yoyo

freely spinning in a cradle rocking move.

# Caddo

Bawl of calf
and feline cough
stark strange
maze of swamp
confirm the dirge
before limp leaf
distorts
and duck wings whirr
in a bateau
in the black trembling
Spanish moss
hands hanging
a wish to cower
and grab for solid
a hold
as forks are
no way divulged
shape and night
collide
in time to paddle
stroke
Caddo maze
of black lace
with diamond eyes
frog croak
smell of rot
swallowing a bateau
in dark diversity.

# Chaining

Ah ah
ahnk
snw.

Winter's loose
in the leaves,
geese
in V's
in the sky —
easy settle
of sleet.

Ah ah
ahnk
snw.

# Is Was Is

A
quick
spiral
going
is
what
is.

Is
reason
for such
a brittle
crunch
of ice
or slice
of it
glittery?

# Desert Mushroom

From there
where cottonwood are fat,
by the parallel tracks of iron
beneath the cloudy mountains,
near the gypsum mounds
appeared that Mushroom.

From
the land of Judge Fountain,
Pat Garrett, Albert Fall,
Oliver Lee,
of six shooters,
dry creeks, ambush
appeared that mushroom,
the first of its kind.

High in the Sacramentos
where clouds spread
among the fir,
cool breezes pushing
the white beauty about,
up and down narrow valley channels,
where rains wash clean
wild raspberries,
and bear and elk move,
there was surprise

that that mushroom was,
that that new thing was there
in the desert
huge,
growing.

# It's a Trade

It's for the good,
asbestos in the walls.
Kill a kid
or two.
Lead in the paint—
have a few
madhatters about.
Spill a little oil—
flip some fish
gill up.
We don't care.
We breathe here,
happy,
full,
sexy.
Let it go.
What's a few, some, or two?
We got more.
Kill a kid or three.

# Yoked

In the dust
and sun
they,
hand to
plow handle,
pushed
pulled
cut the earth
lifted it
curled it
went on
straight
steady
steadily
daily
deadly
on
wearing
into dust

# **Id**entity

How slowly

we earn

our names,

gain the

turns,

curls,

work for swirls,

dot our **I**s.

# Crabtree Amusements, Inc.

Carnival truck —
old work horse —
bug-easy in the pig weed
in the evening heat
Carnival man
—unicorn merchant —
who barked
under the intricate
art of snakes
and spangles
in the weeds
asleep
among curiosities —
four-leaf clovers
and blind mice
with splotched wiry arms
on Indian Paint Brushes
Bluebonnets
ants crawling
on grimy khakis
under the garish
Texas sky.

# Field Hand

Sober blood

bleeds wet

into the dust too

Gardencio chose

to go

hard arm of oak

in the hoe

the sun

slicing through

roll that Black Diamond

down and listen to the

thumping sound

shake of muscle weak

melon in the dirt

seed and pulp.

# Fleeced

Fingers fetch me from
the mound
palms push me about
pummel me soft
make me nice

fit
for service

a chamois
mountain ram
brought down

but I was
I've been
been good bold
been me then
smooth
royally soft

and hard

wafting strong
hooves on stone
muscles tough
ripple swift.

# Matrix

She has spun

the threads of life

into a fine

strong line,

seen herself

in baby eyes.

# Hens

Summer rain clouds,

black setting hens

with angry eyes flashing,

sit on Austin,

tucking the city in

and clucking thunder.

# Poet 1

She sees

the stoop

of the white silk hawk,

rasping beautiful —

a line of taloned life

# Poet 2

Bind a heart

and drive

a word

through it.

# Poet 3

Thrust a lance

into the ice.

Bring forth

Spring.

# Wren Song

I like to go

into the canyons

to find the quick wren

borrow its song,

its moves.

# Las vislumbres sin cesar

Tan fugaz es
en el espejo
la forma que
veo.
Tan fugaz
es el momento
cuando me entra
miedo —
un miedo de
cualquier
soy,
estoy
un miedo de
cualquier
no puedo
jamás
ser,
estar.
El ser que estuve,
el ser que no estaré de nuevo.
¡Soy fugada!

# The Endless Glimpses

So fleeting is
in the mirror
the form
I see.
So fleeting
is the moment
when fear
enters me —
a fear of
whatever
I am,
I am,
a fear of
whatever
I can
never again
be,
be.
The being I am,
the being I will not be again.
I am flown!

# La fiesta

Ahora en San Marcos
una vez mas
el tiempo

de las bayas del enebros
de las bayas gordas, maduras
así

el tiempo
del borrachónes del cielo
del glotónes con alas
estos petirrojos,
estos muchos petirrojos,
estos petirrojos, al parecer,
en todos partes
cayéndose

tropezando
volando dementemente
esparciendo las semillas
del enebros.

# The Fiesta

Now in San Marcos
once again
the time

of the juniper berries
of the fat, ripe berries.
so

the time of the drunkards of the sky
the gluttons with wings
those robins
those many robins
those robins, seemingly
everywhere.
falling down,

stumbling,
flying dementedly
spreading the seeds
 of the juniper.

# Las campanadas

Quisiera hacer un son de madrugada
como los pájaros que charlan en los árboles
tal vez los loros
con sus colores aun charlando —
turquesa, amarillo, rojo,
azul —
mezclando, brillando —
hallándose relámpagos de color
un son
como los gallos
que gritan
rellenos de orgullo
sin miedo
en plumaje rojo
pavoneándose
un son
como las campanas
de las iglesias
que resuenan,
con algunas campanadas
y después
más campanadas,
por fin, viniendo juntamente desde lejos
uniendo

para proclamar
la luz.
Quisiera sonar,
ser,
yo mismo,
un son vivo
un son en la llaneza
de madrugada.

## Bell Sounds

I would like to make a sound of dawn like
the birds that chatter in the trees, per-
haps the parrots with their chattering
colors—turquoise, yellow, red, blue—
mixing, shining—sending out lightning
bolts of color, a sound like the roosters
that shout full of pride, fearless in red
plumage, peacocking—a sound like
the bells of the churches that ring out
with other bells and then more bells fi-
nally coming together from afar uniting
in order to proclaim the light. I would
like to ring out, to be, myself, a sound
alive, a sound in the tranquillity of dawn.

# Rich Man to Lazarus

Strapped for cash

he was

he said

his hands across his waist

his fingers interlaced.

# Une Vue des Oiseaux

Si on peut
entendre
les oiseaux
et
on ne peut pas les voir,
à l'aube
on entendrait le commencement —
la lumière chante,
et
le chanson brille.
Et on commence à sentir,
à  poursuivre
la forme de la source.

## A View of the Birds

If one can hear the birds and not
see them. At dawn one can hear
the beginning — the light  sings
and  the  song  shines  and  one
begins to feel, to follow the form
of the source.

# Cats

We hear the cats of the night
 the many-colored sounds they make
  chant to scream
   a palette of sound

hear the night rise and
 die

touch breast as and
 though they cry

grow more from siren calls
 intense

know and not know why.

# Eagle at Rest

It's the steel

of the ax

that sleeps

quiet

against the earth

and its warm wood

that stretches

archly

toward God.

# Above the Mill Race

We stop
to breathe slow
by the Guadalupe
beneath Gruene's bluff.
We see in the weave of tree

as the pink sun goes
in the water's flow
and silver bounce
see how it is

intricate
quick
momentary

till round the bend
and pink
becomes black.

Yet chill
is the water
and warm the skin
as we breathe slow
by the Guadalupe.

# River Walk

It was warm
soft
winter
the night she said
she was dying.

The river
shivered
with light,
the water
dark
dirty,
her eyes ice.

Mariachis played,
haggled for cash.

# Haida

Neah, Toleah, Sekiu, Kalaloch

Names in the Northwest

sound like water running

Suquamish, Alava, Tatoosh

cascading through rocks

Chetwoot, Lilliwaup, Mukiteo.

I like to hear them

Clallam, Dungeness, Dosewallips,

say them

Skohomish, Wishak, Wynochee, Snohomish

see them written down

Squaxin, Tumwater, Humptulips

see them curling, swirling, churning across the
page

Dewatt, Satsup, Chehalis, Kitsap, Sequim,
Chimacum.

# Notification

The geese
that move above our life
without a honk
are not.

One honk
and vees are glistening
in our light.

# Jollity

Celery, in a stalk,
cattail reaching up,
and slices of melon,
nice day,
just right, soft hair, bronze,
skies high way off up there,
lacey puffs lower
light September breeze, cool
on sun-hot skin
yellow curling mesquite leaves
in a spider web,
some solid shade from live oaks,
and a crawler or two,
no buzzes, thank goodness,
no sound really, not even her breath,
and she so here
with me heavy on the pallet,
sinking in deep

# Up in it

She can't fly

thinks she can though

thinks she's gull high

loose

fluff and go

thermal stuff

caught light

albatross

and hummingbird —

her way of doing

# Schooled

Oozey stuff
gets waffled
becomes flat
static
gets pressed
patterned
fitted neatly
gets made acceptable
digestible
loses its bubble
flow
won't stick to
fingers
loses its
ooze.

# Relatively Speaking

Myopic minions of time
gribble across,
eliptically.
As ants do move,
or songs, counterpunctually.
Fogged in too, unperceiving of the
forms encased in gray so nearby,
and hand and arm outstretched seeking,
nose sniffing, ears too keen for shape
yet late and early, the winding of time
moves near
unavailingly
for no sense is there to gather in such motion,
such dancing, such purity.
Some say time's bent.
Others say straight, even symmetrical.
None know, certainly, but
fluctuate, I say — warp
and woof and wane and freeze
like Wile Coyote hanging in

space.

# Big Gil's Clientele

The smoke's thick,
burns my eyes,
the beer's hot and high.
I don't see no girls.
My blue jeans is tight,
hurts my gut,
music's too loud,
popcorn's in my teeth.
Too dark to see
them girls even if
they come back,
but did you see
them knockers
and them tight pants.
Sure like to have me some of that.
Whooeey, give me
another beer.

## To the Numbers

We dance daily,
not gaily
but jumping about
with a hurly burly here
and scurry there,
in and out,
one, two, three,
left, right, left.

Yes, we dance;
to the caller's demands
we move,
in step, according to plan,
just so and so just,
we move
til', at last, the music stops,
and we stand sweating,
disengaged,
feeling our aching everything,
and wonder, "Will it begin again,
or was that last number
'Good Night, Irene'?"